WHY DOES MY BODY DO THAT?

BURP

by Rachel Rose

Consultant: Beth Gambro
Reading Specialist, Yorkville, Illinois

Minneapolis, Minnesota

Teaching Tips

Before Reading

- Look at the cover of the book. Discuss the picture and the title.

- Ask readers to brainstorm a list of what they already know about burps. What can they expect to see in this book?

- Go on a picture walk, looking through the pictures to discuss vocabulary and make predictions about the text.

During Reading

- Read for purpose. Encourage readers to think about burps as they are reading.

- Ask readers to look for the details of the book. What are they learning about the body and how it burps?

- If readers encounter an unknown word, ask them to look at the sounds in the word. Then, ask them to look at the rest of the page. Are there any clues to help them understand?

After Reading

- Encourage readers to pick a buddy and reread the book together.

- Ask readers to name two things that can cause burps. Find the pages that tell about these things.

- Ask readers to write or draw something they learned about burps.

Credits: Cover and title page, © Ranta Images/iStock and © CHUNYIP WONG/iStock; 3, © karelnoppe/iStock; 5, © MIA Studio/Shutterstock; 6, © Prostock-Studio/iStock; 6–7, © monkeybusinessimages/iStock; 8, © Roman Yanushevsky/Shutterstock; 11, © yodiyim/iStock and © Krakenimages.com/Shutterstock; 13, © kool99/iStock; 14, © combomambo/iStock; 14–15, © nednapa/Shutterstock; 17, © SDI Productions/iStock; 18–19, © SolStock/iStock; 20–21, © wat/iStock and © ferrantraite/iStock; 22, © Tetiana Lazunova/iStock; 23TL, © SrdjanPav/iStock; 23TR, © Weedezign/iStock; 23BL, © Ranta Images/iStock; 23BC, © DigitalSoul/iStock; and 23BR, © yodiyim/iStock.

Library of Congress Cataloging-in-Publication Data

Names: Rose, Rachel, 1968- author.
Title: Burp / by Rachel Rose.
Description: Minneapolis, Minnesota : Bearport Publishing Company, [2023] |
    Series: Why does my body do that? | Includes bibliographical references
    and index.
Identifiers: LCCN 2022023092 (print) | LCCN 2022023093 (ebook) | ISBN
    9798885093354 (library binding) | ISBN 9798885094573 (paperback) | ISBN
    9798885095723 (ebook)
Subjects: LCSH: Belching--Juvenile literature. | Digestion--Juvenile
    literature. | Human physiology--Juvenile literature.
Classification: LCC QP145 .R59 2023 (print) | LCC QP145 (ebook) | DDC
    612.3--dc23/eng/20220611
LC record available at https://lccn.loc.gov/2022023092
LC ebook record available at https://lccn.loc.gov/2022023093

Copyright © 2023 Bearport Publishing Company. All rights reserved. No part of this publication may be reproduced in whole or in part, stored in any retrieval system, or transmitted in any form or by any means, electronic, mechanical, photocopying, recording, or otherwise, without written permission from the publisher.

For more information, write to Bearport Publishing, 5357 Penn Avenue South, Minneapolis, MN 55419.

Contents

A Funny Sound 4

See It Happen 22

Glossary 23

Index 24

Read More 24

Learn More Online..................... 24

About the Author 24

A Funny Sound

I eat my lunch very quickly.
Then, something happens.
Buuurrp!
Why does my body do that?

Everyone burps.

Grown-ups and kids do it.

Babies do, too.

How do burps start?

Burps begin when there is too much **gas** in your **stomach**.

Your body needs to get rid of some gas!

The **muscles** around your stomach **squeeze** and let go.

This pushes the extra gas out.

It leaves your mouth as a burp.

How does gas get into your stomach?

It happens when you swallow air.

A lot of air comes in when you eat quickly!

Fizzy drinks can make you burp a lot, too.

These drinks have little gas bubbles in them.

Pop, pop, pop!

Some burps are quiet.

Others are very loud!

Remember to say excuse me after you burp.

17

How can you burp less?

Slow down when you eat or drink.

Try not to talk when you eat.

Talking brings in extra air.

There is nothing wrong with burping.

Some people burp up to 30 times a day!

Have you burped yet today?

Buuurrp!

See It Happen

Burps start when your stomach has too much gas.

Muscles squeeze and let go to push some gas out.

The gas travels from your stomach up to your mouth.

It leaves your body as a burp.

22

Glossary

fizzy filled with tiny bubbles

gas something like air with no shape

muscles parts of the body that help you move

squeeze to press something tightly

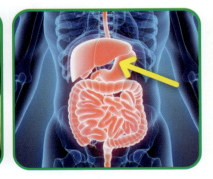

stomach the part of the body that breaks down food

Index

bubbles 14
eating 4, 12, 18
gas 9–10, 12, 14, 22
mouth 10, 22
muscles 10, 22
stomach 9–12, 22

Read More

Hansen, Grace. *Burps (Beginning Science: Gross Body Functions).* Minneapolis: Abdo Kids, 2021.

Hughes, Sloane. *My Stomach (What's Inside Me?).* Minneapolis: Bearport Publishing, 2022.

Learn More Online

1. Go to **www.factsurfer.com** or scan the QR code below.
2. Enter "**Burp**" into the search box.
3. Click on the cover of this book to see a list of websites.

About the Author

Rachel Rose lives in California. She doesn't really like it when people burp loudly, but she thinks it's funny when her dog does!